Oregon
Winter

OREGON WINTER

by

JEANNE McGAHEY

WOOLMER/BROTHERSON Ltd.
Andes, New York

1973

The following poems first appeared in *Poetry: Recurrent Dream, Poem for January, Refusal for Heaven,* and *That Lately Shone* (originally called *Ballad*).

The following poem first appeared in *WORKS, a quarterly of writing: Remembering Robert Frost.*

The following poems first appeared in "Five Young American Poets, Second Series," New Directions, 1942: *Oregon Winter, Story About The Dead, But Going Up We Lost That, Descent Out Of Mountains, When I Have Seen In Hills, Street With People, Year With Wars,* and *Warning by Daylight.*

Library of Congress Card Number: 73-76689

Contents

PART 1
SCENE BY RECOLLECTION

OREGON WINTER

The rain begins.   This is no summer rain
Dropping the blotches of wet on the dusty road:
This rain is slow, without thunder or hurry:
There is plenty of time—there will be months of rain.

Lost in the hills, the old gray farmhouses
Hump their backs against it, and smoke from their chimneys
Struggles through weighted air.   The sky is sodden with water,
It sags against the hills, and the wild geese,
Wedge-flying, brush the heaviest cloud with their wings.

The farmers move unhurried.   The wood is in,
The hay has long been in, the barn lofts piled
Up to the high windows, dripping yellow straws.
There will be plenty of time now, time that will smell of fires,
And drying leather, and catalogues, and apple cores.

The farmers clean their boots, and whittle, and drowse.

STORY ABOUT THE DEAD

Wave pulling the long weeds backward:
Sag and haul of tide
Out of the cave of shells:
                              O drag of it down hills.

All night I heard the goats come down from the bracken
To try the bitter water:
Noise of their slotted feet
Among the agates:
                              Out of the dark their eyes
Show over the clump of bells.

In the fog I remember
The lovers and the dead: the dead and the lovers:
How in the slide and slip
Of sand out of a shut-up hand, have I remembered
The touching of cold hair.

                              O lovers:
In the morning the women pick up driftwood,
Pile it along their arms.   They walk by the water.
Their heels leave sockets in the sand.

How shall I say by this,
Memory, memory, like a water-bell,
Like the sea-blowing smell of caverns.
. . . Under some swing
Of finger-long leaves they are the lifted deer:
The three-pointed swallows:
Touched with the break of glass:
                              (and brushing the bright bees
Caught breath in, said "My love.")

Or shall I say, in the morning the women come

To the rock pool for shells: their hands among the kelp
Shutting the fingering sea-flowers.

Shall I say, the springs break out of the rocks:
The cliffs have the long stains.

                              The women look
Through their blown hair, or under the palms of their hands
At the fisherman: the salmon shine like buckets.

The air is full of spray and the windy smoke.

RECURRENT DREAM

We were by water
Clear with light:
              the sun making the pebbles round.
I felt your mouth
The many wings flying
All my blood
Beginning the storm of bees.
The touch of everything that time
Was like the edge of flowers
              Or I held
Between my hands as between book pages
The believed bird.
              Oh wing and the small bones
Hollow light and the wildness.

And the dream stopped.
              But I remember,
But I carry always
In my palm the fear
The moving of feathers
The quick eyes.

WHEN I HAVE SEEN IN HILLS

When I have seen in hills the smoky rain:
Walked in it, past the hedges giving up birds,
This is the rain
I thought would not come back.
                              Looking at sky
A clutter of stars, I have said, "Permit this":
And the knuckle of pipe
Dry at the watering place,
The field having, since the cloudy dandelions
Nothing for flowers:
Now easily in so many places
The stems of rain
And rattle of water somewhere.
                              The branches
Weighing as if with apples.
                              And not remembered
Except as striking with your hand
An old bell, to leave the metal whining.

BUT GOING UP WE LOST THAT

But going up we lost that:
                              how the mountain
Turned such tall sky to stone.
                                   But being here
Among the near rocks, there is such gleaming
As must be new in wings of dragon flies
And in each pine point separately, and in the wind
With leaves laid out upon it,
                              and those long
Far-blowing threads the spiders go by.
                                        And the lake
By day has sparkle and shaking of an aspen side,
By night turns up such stars
You can lay hand to in the downward dark.

DESCENT OUT OF MOUNTAINS

Back to the tame water and the smudged stars,
Being not brave enough for mountains.   The sun's last heat
Fades from the chilling granite, terrible with cold
The high peaks wait alone, the hills draw in
Like stone doors closing.
Back to the walled meadows and the soft rain,
Being not great enough for mountains.   Leave the tree
Stricken with autumn, the torrent sharp with ice,
The black bear heavy with sleep.
                              Those alone
With metal in their bones, the quiet men
Tolerant of the long cold and the late spring.
The frozen bird and the branch broken by snow
Are not rejected now, cast out of the high places.

AT THE VOICE OF A BIRD

So died
(all but the day-blue eyes)
not willing.

A dozen hours
we heard that heart, that big and muscular
long-loved Percheron
plodding the mindless dark
                              (Viola, mother)
and the lungs cry in and out
like a hail-shaped harp.

And the light came
gray as a level,
the smell of a bitter weed,
and the whole cold Pacific
gathered its lunge and tilt
and swung at the buoy and poured toward Labrador—
oh high on the toss caught the lark
of the seventeenth summer—
so bell-bold,
a heart's whole walkaway

And she that came to the window
the darling of birds
a thrush's memory.

And Margaret also.

I remember
forest, and the walking, delicate-pointed,
shadow-making deer: those children:

Trillium cold the small five-fingered hands:

In sandals we walked beside the bending wheat
and full of tidings.

Over us high the sun's untouchable daisy
and the night coming soon
in brute-shaped shadows.

Once on an evening
scary with stars
and humming all about
we went through the minted orchard
through gates that squealed like lambs,
saw in the twilight that gray casket
Margaret-shaped
with terror in its eyeballs.

Dead and dead she sat
(all but the day-blue eyes
of the lost children).

They will not appear in the time of the yellow star
the smoke of the pipes of the uncles
will never call them home
nor the bruising apples.
                  But on that hillside
(the lark could not possibly sing on any other)
the snake will shudder away, the locust
withdraw his coupled, gay and calisthenic leg.

Oh, here's a death, Lord,
lay thy liddy hand
upon this myrrh, this may, this vining myrtle

thy shadow like an aster:

But all of the children
are running here like the air-remembering water.
Bare bushes will spring with leaves . . . and even the heart
that rocks in anyone's chest
its sunless and murmuring chambers:
                              Viola, Margaret
the small wigged birds are coming: they sing at all the fences
(Oh by this winter's briar's gate
so easterly rise up!)

                    Narrow as flutes
they hang along the wires. Their small barbed feet
are dry.
          They catch like crickets.

BURIAL PLACE

Among these rocks dry generations of the lichen
            and that dear
Raw orchid of the flesh about to abandon bone
In stillness no loud machine may enter, or lark converse with
Reminds us we are mourners.

The teams go off down the hill, colleague by colleague,
Sober, the wide backs wagging:
            and we who are left here frightened
In our silks, lean speaking of the dead as of begonias.

Now we count losses by buds, or as drear chattel
Heavily charged for:
            whatever daylight may return us
As consolation, tool or other makeshift
Solid beneath a sky
Neither raining nor without its leaf
We are the celebrants
This moment will bitterly not pardon
Its weeping sleeve, its flower of stalk and horn.

OLD CEMETERY

A still fog from the near sea coming
To damp these lichens; to cool the century-clean
Old stones.
   Silent here, so long the moss has laid
One feather on another. I think how the skulls
Are breakable slight hollows, and the slow earth
Closing there like sleep: the roots of pines
Alternate with the cool long bones.

In April in the early and beaded spring
They come here, love in their knees: disturbed
And brilliant touching. They hear the water turning
And the wind over stones, and the wave's pulled going-out
Loose in the pebbles. The cedar smell
From the cut boughs goes by them.

And they are valuable
As otters or the glitter of bees:
But after a little while are not together.

Being alone and watching the sea changing
The beach of my footprints. Going down to it.
Finding an ivoried agate in a litter of shells
And laying it cool and whole in my palm's hollow.
And a clear bird turning in narrow wings,
The fog closing it. And no sound anywhere
But foghorn and the sea's noise.

EVENING AFTER HEAT

With that late color of sun on the blond hills
The oaks long-shadow the pale straw.

And the strawberry pickers go home to the fruit camps
Under the split willows.   The sun dark in their skins.

                    Their girls are quiet
For the heat still shaking the hill:
Their eyes are like an evening.

The fruit camp on the bank of the flat river
And the melon smell of water:
The big frogs in the shallows belling the narrow moon.

And the dark comes then,
And is a fear perhaps, or a sleeping:
Or they hear the edge of the river going among the tules,
Or watch the stars slide under the little boats.

SKIN DIVER

Those on some beach
Indelicate in sun, and leggy with long girls:
In rows they sleep
Their hides loved up in brown
While hauls and pulls
Soundless the bitter old Pacific.

Who will see waterly the skyline and its scooting sail?
What changes is close in.   The elbow tans and turns,
the eyelight flickers like a fish.

Enter the water, dolphin or brother:
This costume like a clown
Makes credible
Invasions airless and comic.   The gassy weed is lifted
And the fish come pushing their noses
Like so many elbows:
Do we sight-see here
Among the deft, the fingerless, the lucky?
Are we the visionary, unattended, lost,
Where the starfish locks and shines,
                              the halibut
Is sliding his bone's row home?

SCENE BY RECOLLECTION

Not anyone, by highway, turn of tide,
By town, by tower, by lantern's look,
By the gulls all crying like watchmen
Shall return:

The children rose up out of the seagrass
With the sound of a thousand swallows.
(O where are the marks that were left
At the water's cold edge?)
                    In the swamps
They hunted as tigers the marguerites
(But will not be found there now by fours and fives
In the dry trails.)

All night over the reef an ocean rolled its barrels
All day Sunday the Fords went by like pickets.

The dead have been carried past so many bridges,
All following their heels:
So many dying: the eyes like terriers
Or a bird's departure:
Call up the diggers' shapes of old umbrella,
Look no way back, Oh keeper of this cold gable.

Not any one by angel, not by steel
By stone returns: the foghorn will blow all night
Like a cold animal,
No spaniel rise up on his stick bones.
The children among the dunes

Hear if they hear it the spring like a gabriel coming
Lark on a post his klaxon
But turn as crocus no more, return no more.

Oh herald, howler at night, horn-hurling wind out of Arago
Shake as a host those rafters.
That old military storm gone south
Rides no rail backward.

Not any can hurry the sound of its high wheels.

NOVEMBER NORTHERN

And the horses come about
Obedient: lonely the faces
Like long knees swing,
And the sower tilts in the hail
His stinging hand.

In the gravel where all my dead are buried
Someone more strange is walking:
Like a bent brother or a remote, short-fingered doll.
Visitors, what are you doing—
Those who disturb me no longer
With fell smiling?

At west the light descends
(The unenduring, that dearly, you fool, you love):

Companion by dark companion
The crows are leaving us.   In this air
So stained with iodine you know your losses
Greater than all you owned.
This cold coming out of the north
With a dry wasp and a Yankee salt of scorn
Is unable, as you, to pardon.
I to these winds have given
What could ill be spared:
To deny impossible,
And to absolve, too late.

PART 2
YEAR WITH WARS

THE GATES WE LEFT

The gates, the gates we left
    when we broke the city.
Did we leave no guard, no animal grave and wasted,
Not anyone any use to us?
Nobody lovely, with anything in his pockets
Or able to speak of doves
    did we leave no one?

YEAR WITH WARS

Sometimes among their winds and lions
Surprise the boneless fauns: (Here is my hand
O all the perfumes of Arabia
Could not sweeten): how the pigeons stare
Out of the circles of their eyes.

It is the year, the year of the fields of asters.
The ants walk in a rope
Under the crosses of the stars.   The boys go into the towns,
Carry the guns like stems of palms
Like blue or breakable platters: and lie down to sleep
Anywhere.   (But remembering sails and olives.)

In the daylight, crossing the marshes,
I saw the frogs that were up to their eyes in water;
Then all the ghosts got up that were among the cattle,
Knocking the bells with knuckles.
Afterward I thought of the dead with their hands like pencils.

Sometimes there is a smoke like morning in the fields:
The windows shine all night in the frosty apples.
It is the year, I said,
The year of the bees.   They dig for honey
In the locusts, or in the fruiter's shop
are thick as berries.   But the soldiers have death
For their keepsake.   Pile up rocks
To show where the place was.   Or they stop at the river,
Holding their caps for nothing
To look at the swarm with the penny-colored wings.

NOTES ON A BATTLE

Heard the wind
Pouring its length
Down a sky like an absolute stranger.
Weather will come of this:
                          and did come travel.
Surveyor, to gape with a single optic:
(Maker of any acre
Out of our named one?)
Came other:
              the scavenner: Old Bottom with his bull's head,
And traffic among corpses.

Look to the witch I cried
And got to my hayrick.
                      In the saltmarsh
She appears.   In the cow-encircling hills
That rigrag Goldilocks and with her bat-wide smile
Insomniac rides.

Go make a holiday, who hear this:
Write it on big boards, fill papers up
With news we were defeated.
                          Call up the kin
From their ingles:
                  Smith from his smoky ingots:
Frederick: and thirty Margarets shall ride
With a readable banner.

But one must go by the bridge
The home of the eyeless goat
(Perpetual wanderer)
Grip like a handful of aster

That ropy and hideous hide.

I will walk three times
Past the worm in the corn:
I will count my own in a lingo absolute.
And calling that land Toledo,
By rail available,
                    ah furious with victory will climb
To the hill in the drying meadow.

Crickets will sing
About us like crooked birds.
The night with its many humors
Hap gently our three angels.

Firmament like an Eldorado will be upon us,
Under our heels our earth's broad biscuit.

This is my name and occupation.
If there is other
Must look, look long, and to a longer county.

Knowing these waxes soon undone
Dare grant them this one unlingering—
(Death my persuasion and admittance,
My door's darling)—
Never a long time love.

FAMILY CIRCLE

Who in the dark beneath the hallway clocks, holding
the anklebone of some small crying cannibal, does not
remember how he came here: headlong as a fish, without a
coat or language except that terrible vowel that rises
from his jaws like some well-oiled and nimble engineer:

The nursery. Its government by syntax. The small
meat of his person indexed and suitably dried. And the
eye like a bald assassin's wish for public approval.

Here on this map of continents where the wry nations
sit, the salt floods swing like ironware, where slides
the shark his single and frigid shoulder—here among
walls of glass that click and shine, where briefly the
private grudges take the shape of home—here is the dim
heart hunted, odorless and without footprint. Shall the
leopard enter without scab? The mantis renounce her grip
and deadly jowl?

Within the savage halo of their care, where he lies
public, plucked and smiled upon: condemned to love the
first large mammal that eyes him in his sleep—he is
alive without poultices. As a small journey by auto,
innocent. As a house rid of its stranger.

Above his head the great palms close and open. The
hundred English verbs for saying no.

And the pelicans fly south with the backs of angels.

Do you want him to hear that rush of Baltic waters?
Do you want him to wake up some day and find out who he

is? Do you want looking down on us all some great sane
Eye?

Dolphin, she said. (And great-aunt Ida's hairpiece
loose in the cold-stream wind.) *Where does he think he's
going, bare and humped like a cub?*

I've made mistakes, she said: *and love's the easiest
killed. But the heart's a tough mutton. Hear how it goes
on beating.*

And wept in the failing light.

THE DOLLS

The people in that country all were smiling.
All counted each other for sleep.
                              Agreeably walked
On an afternoon past windows less than sixty.
Hearts having the weight of bonnets or blue stones
Beat from the left all day.

These do not enter the forest between the judas trees.
On the plateau
Do not hunt the tall animals with the lions' heads—
For their undoing
Have the dolls, dear bodkins.
                              No long beast howling
Is enemy in that country.

Enemy lies at the heart's small drums and winches:
Is nimble, spry on its wires,
Has hands like the narrow hands of a frog,
Is cupboard sleeper, killer.
                              At midnight the minikin armies
Deliver the scheduled ruin.

And one down that avenue enormous
Between two mirrors ran clapping like a shoe.
One whispered about his love
To the black confessor.
                              One followed the drowned
With a tourniquet of roses.

And one who was named in that country

The name of an animal,
Tornado, inventor, beast-crosswise,
Died there, heart split like a hare.

Lidless they lie along the loving arm
Lighter than wigs of silk.
                    So waits the serpent's
Chill and smiling head:
                    the spider
Who turns (upon the caught) small spinning hands
And his severe and complicated strangler's eye.

STREET WITH PEOPLE

At all the corners,
Feeling out nickels in their pockets.
                    Holding the packages
The shape of wheels or loaves: in windows
Themselves among the bowls and knives.

                    O travellers,
Spread out the pages spotted with periods.
The children with kites
Are running between the hills,
The sky is hauling them up
To the ends of their arms: the wind is blowing
The straight leaves.

But they are old, the travellers.
Their eyes like grapes: their nickel eyelids:
They are walking in fives among the telephones,
They are winding their thumbs like spools,
They are buttoning their coats with knuckles.

It is too late now
To go looking for the lovers
In the skillet dark: the unbuckling hands,
The body shape of an X, the pellet nipples:
It is too late now to listen for their humming like coins.

What is the time, O lovers, travellers?
The watches tick in the cuff,
The dark is among the posts,
The night drops down in sparrows.

It is the evening of the stars returning like cornices.
To the Chryslers and the women with umbrellas
The stars are coming back like nails.

FUNERAL FOR A HEAD

The funeral, that zero smile
They wired you with, like some awful bouquet—
Do you think I am fooled?   Do I think you are any more dead
Because of a cooler house?

Lady who stood in the doorway calling the flies,
Ancient, untalented, unrenewable,
That other queen, the one who died of you,
Whose daughter sleeps,
They celebrate your spindle:
Its destruction among bluer flowers.

Disguised as young
You kept the old hearts buzzing:
(Smooth, smooth the jowl):
                              disguised as kin—
Small ladylike hands of hornet
And sly the poking eye—
I think it was Orestes spoke of murder
As if it were a key.

Now in this masquerade
So utterly becoming—flesh of hyacinth
And formalin: It can hardly be said to sleep
What winters in your shadow
Confronted by inertias,
Small, friable and stunned.

POEM FOR JANUARY

Now in this January
    that old toad disaster
Grinning between his heels like a chill fable,
Calamity in the streets
Being yelled by boys
    (and yet, not yet,
Not ever, so they say, so brutal, drummed and damned
As our own ragbag derelict dismay.)

Few enough speak of love in this butcher's weather:
Destruction a masterpiece,
The mad among us, spreading like indigo,
All starred, scarred, terrified,
Hound-hindered, whining:
      now in this January
In this leper's congress
Take this word gently:
Hold it as some oval
Low immense inviolable city:
This widow's walk of a winter
Whatever its kill and kill
Returns (or shall return?)
That perilous high
That candelabraed high, most agate head,
Those horns akimbo.

The loved small animals
Shall emerge as marigolds,
      and in the yellow air
The living birds in dozens
Sing all the names of the Persians.

This rusty, cold, this cross-begotten sky,
Creak open and let by lordship
Arcturus down
    across the postal zones.

REMEMBERING ROBERT FROST

The old and dishevelled may well take aim.
Whatever they came for: the lucky fix,
The absolute noise, the smile that disappeared
Like a sparrow:
                    these being forfeit
Leave little to lose.
Let them take up such sidearms then
As the young being made awkward by promises
Had better leave not handled.

The tall who have improved by accident,
More lovely than the crane with elbows
And starving like the dove:
                    these no Adversary
Can get much hold on:
                    or his lightless face endure.

LINES FOR A FIFTY-FIFTH BIRTHDAY

I passed the doctor busy with his hemps, I
      called him from his wounding.
Sir, I cried, and caught the small bright
      muscle of his eye.
Bring halters, poultices,
The several inhabitants of the body, the
      unspeakable organs,
They falter, the greases drain away, and the
      stone forms in the bile
Like a bitter jewel, and the luck is out.

The goat said long ago, the lion said,
King's X, this would not happen;
And a voice far off,
Any spirit involved among these tendons
Like a jugged hare in a pot,
It has only to speak.

But the years arriving
Were not informed. Here came the pages tattling,
Here came the postman stamping like half a horse,
And I, poor animal, not ringed about with unicorns
Or any doves to flap like a Monday wash
Now in the wind from that most ungainly north
So stand and stiffen:
Deformity neither scarred nor blest,
Forsworn but not foreseen.

PART 3
FANTASY FOR PLANET

SEA SERPENT

Where shall he walk?
On the berry-colored salt and atlas sea.
Who shall his crony be?
                              Not any.
Who shall leige him?
                              None . . .
No not my love, my lord lion, stalking
                              at timberline
His large and meadow-wandering kill:
And his weed shall be
                              of oriole.

Old fogies in the rusty weather
Dream for a dram or two
                    that kelpy
Locomotive length:
                    and the legless complains to his boot
How the gone bone aches
                    (and god knows in what hallway
Of haik or crail).

Ahab, Ahab,
Rager over the blue-bell perilous water
After mild whales—
Where's among you
The one with an eye like the private device of a lord,
The hand nine minutes late?

A lubber he climbs to his crow's tree:
Fumbling lines:
                    with a hitch at his heel
And a ho in his throat
For a stranger—
But he hears a whine from the north
Like a Dutchman's hail

And the slack sea heaves like a tub,
And he turns
            and ah beholds
As if his eyes were agates
That great rearhorse
Rise from his glory hole—
                    lift up
His high Iberian head
With the immense curled horn
And hurling a wake of larks
So move on Britain!

Later he walks the dry and hilly deck
As one returned from a cape or an ambush
With an odd anger:
              his shadow bends at his heel
And marked by holystone.

And the whales go by in couples—the warehouse brow
The merry eye like a mayflower.
                Daily he calls their blow.
But ever the sea's wide ring retreats
And he follows after:
And the dolphins follow his mark upon the water.

ULYSSES

On the sea where only the tailed and chilly
Are awake, the traveller, aimless,
Salty, stiff as a shank
Has heard the sirens singing like charwomen.
There on their fireless rock
(Small clutches of salt and horn)
Sits splendid Helen, grudging,
Who spent a city
Waiting some slumberous, vast, wrong-headed hero.

His fingers are pickled in brine as cucumbers are, or gudgeons:
Odysseus: behind him doll-dark Circe.
The beast of the sea encircles him like a harp.
He parts his beard lying: Which way home?

But the sea scuffles and slides:
His prow like a sick bird turns
Not toward that dry and underflowering coast;
And somewhere eastward, windless
The sun with his head of bright bone, implacable, rises.

JOURNEY

Down, down his days goes
Like emigrant, or believer.

At the name that cannot be spelled
Hails stranger: what is this place?
Receives no answer.

    Shoulder by shoulder the relatives
    Walk together like two in fog.
               In the valley
    The waters spout and spring: pass by:
    The wells are marked
    With the double bone.
                  If you go as far as the tall house
    Take a messenger.
              The orchards dangle with bells:
    Pass by: The cities also.

O tall surveyor, mourner, counter of coins,
Fearing the guant old woman and the second-hand man:
Fearing the cat that will appear two colors,
And the dead man under the gables
Who should have been destroyed in August . . .

Where do the six trails go?   What are the mountains named
That are colored like Iroquois?   What tilting Danubes
Pour out their primrose?

    Shoulder by shoulder the relatives
    Are turning their heads like bundles.
    They carry the charms: the key like an ace,
    The terrier, the crooked puzzle:
    Comfort themselves with the old diseases
    Darling as brooches.

48

O book-maker, holder of crosses like cones
The hangman waits beside his pendulum: beside his pools
The cruel miller: *Are the plains all crossed*
By the dark meridians? Is the cleated panther
Awake among his hills?

Down down his days goes
Like spy or unbeliever: in the rusty valley
The big bones lying like tools:

                           Are the crows forbidden
Here?   Are the serpents destroyed
In the Tetons?   What follows, follows,
Howls like an old machine at traveller?

Receives no answer.

WHO SHOWS US THE FACE OF GOD

Who shows us the face of God like a broad door: the key
That nowhere lies, not in our limping muscle, not in the rings
Of angels laughing with silver teeth and those great crutchy wings;
He terribly halts before us.   How shall he be
Our stem and stalk, our stop?   At his crippled knee
We like small violets clutching, and the hornet sings
Of murder.   We remember horses, and the kings
With the imperfect shadows, and the dull returning sea.

Image before us: absolute: the broken nail
We hang upon, whose faltering and stubborn cry
Is our only word: what makes us drive
And wander where all the customs fail
But watching among ravens the beasts that die
And the morning light that finds us still alive.

CATHEDRAL WITH IMAGES

Above her head a halo of armless birds:
On candlewax she ascends, like a paper pigeon:
Without luggage, hallooing among the clouds.

Lady, this grove of windy rafters,
High in the groin the gaudy colt of heaven,
His wrists broken like dowels—
Even the stones have faces:
The carp, the mayfly and the chinless parrot.

I will burn a candle like a small albino
For the lovers who part sometimes like flowering curtains:
For the dead, the women with white tongues
And the small peculiar heads of bees.

                    Lady from whose eyelids
The tears descend like artifacts,
When down the hallway stalks the great engine
Like an unbending and English-speaking horse—
Remember Christopher:
                    us also:
Who came not looking for luck, or any Saint Curative,
But searching as old dogs do
A likeness found too late:
Or in the large plain faces of the paralyzed.

REFUSAL FOR HEAVEN

As for that furniture
Bloodied and dreaded
That waits on the mound
Like a one-foot watcher—
Admire admire
Those jacks on a stick
That mount
Go up like a rope-trick—

                    heaven's their ho.

But I was the one, remember,
Howled for no haven,
                 did ever love this local
L-shaped acre, this, this willow,
Budded and birded, the shadows passing
On grasses of those I loved.

O tell yourself (try telling)
This rickrack skeleton
All jury-rigged with filaments
Eager to shriek's no matter:
A throwaway card, a pickaback rider,
A rucksack, random-coupled,
Pegged out with ailments like a pound of nails . . .

By all its locks, blocks, all its luckless errand
O by this or any
Trick sly half a self in a mirror
Return, return!

Whatever the center is, heart maybe,
That the live love lives, a cameo,
A seascape, or some belt-wide blade
Wedged, edged and entered—
Return say the watchers:
Approach as the beetle his love
With genuflections of spry wires
Or the small kept ticking
Of a wristbone:

Disturb the gods with questions.
We are only a stone's throw from a cloud,
From the look of a people who rise like a spinning jenny's
Remarkable leak from heaven.

                    O lords and ladies
Of valuable cargo
Consider that what we know is random:
The truth is waiting for any
That has a leg out of key
Or a likeness posted in his forehead
(Let not you name it)—
A touch too simple
To be arranged for.

But we must go, must go
A carter's journey to a tipperary:
Hob's mare to lead us,
Anger our next of kin,
Our sweet unspeakable dolly.
            (O if love were the likeliest linnet
Other shall queenlier rage!)

What shall I tell

My wraithy and furious selves?

He will wear
                 (It is said in Scotland)
A tree on his head,
A rack like a hat of thorn:
                              ah surely in that hour
Another I (some lovelier luckstruck
I still I) shall hear my name called wholly.

Voices shall be about us like waterbirds.
The crane and the heron
Shall dance for us their broomstick
Gentle almost flying love—
Shall rise to flail like a harvest.

And the air shall shout with their wings,
                      and the white
Unwounding feathers shall fly like a Hail Mary.

THAT LATELY SHONE

Of the flesh that lately shone
Disabuse the comic bone.

From the scowling ape of skin
Liberate the angel sin.

Who never lived let him also die
Of the ailment communal and sly.

Agent he was and never other
Never the self but the brother.

For him who celebrates his fall
Prepare those mansions cold and tall.

And she that never will be wed
Double lies in her single bed.

She that never was his bride
Let her go on a journey wide.

Give to her hands a golden key
And let her climb the gallows tree.

Hang up the rakestraw in the corn
And crown it with a crow of thorn.

Break the cornflower from its stem
And tell the way to Bethlehem.

And still the love he never knew
Will bar the passage of the shrew.

Dig the earth and turn it deep
And may she sleep and may she sleep.

WARNING BY DAYLIGHT

This is the corner, look four ways at stone:
Watch in two streets a wind
In the rattled and paper autumn.
      (This to be dreamed of,
In some dark waken and hear the heart strike fear.)

Pages against the grating
Turn war and the Katzenjammers, someone named Talbot
Or merchandise.
      She leaned out from a window,
Held apart curtains.
      I saw her face
True Romances, the hair yolk-yellow,
And the pearls lay out
On the tight satin, and she held a cup
That was blue and empty: and whatever it was she said,
Or whether she laughed, I saw her mouth move with it,
Dental and bright.
      But it was the stone I heard
And gutter of leaves.
      And seeing how the wind
Blew big the curtains, and her red-cluttered hand
Twisted the cord, even before I woke
I saw she was the death that I had come for.

FANTASY FOR PLANET

We have run everywhere
As if we were on stalks:
We have covered our human track
With the dragged shape of a hare—
And still no hider, none anonymous, never the lucky.

The palm with its crosses warned us,
Spelled out our names in X's.
                              In Egypt, in islands
In the shade of the leaning heads
We have laid out the cards,
We have bowed down like anvils:
Deliver us.

We went to market without a ring or thimble:
There sat the survivors, knitting.
Old Jonathan rose up, told time by strangers,
Held oyster like a little brain—
Then passed by daylight
The dry watchman.

We went to war:
The guns all rubbed with a mutton bone,
The corporals tall:
And who in the blizzard battle hid from the general,
Who at the well-curb fell—
None pardoned, none return.

We are the ones who are riding one way
The horse of an uncertain fever:

Who have eaten already the oak.
                              Dark, dark the starling
That snaps the stinging fly.
                              And dry the bitter vetch.
Ever there ticks in the wall
                              the beetle like an Elgin.
                              Ever there loosens

From his twig
The gray and windy thrush.

And he who lies down living,
And hopes perhaps to rise:
Who turns his spotted eye
Up toward an amaze of planets—
For a hook, a crook, some ladder, latch—
For some great god-fist
To draw him gaping up
Shouting hozannas and shaking like a cod—

Must cut his losses first.
                              These being absolute.

58